CCSS Genre Fiction

M000305686

Essential Question
What do we love about animals?

Ava's Animals

by Anita Rodriguez
illustrated by George Hamblin

Chapter 1: **All About Animals**

"Okay, class," said Mr. Edson. "Today you'll have time to work on your poster of your favorite animal. Remember, it should show the animal's habitat, and you can use the computer to find pictures."

Ava loved animals, so she was excited about her new assignment. There was just one problem. She liked too many different animals! She was supposed to have picked one for her poster by now, but she couldn't decide.

"I love lots of animals," thought Ava, "and I want my poster to express that. Maybe looking at someone else's project will give me ideas."

"Which animal did you choose?" she asked her friend Ruth.

"Here, take a look," Ruth said. She passed Ava a small stack of pictures she'd printed from the computer.

3

Ava flipped through the pictures. Each one was different, but they all showed beavers. Some were splashing in the water, while others were scraping bark off trees with their big beaver teeth. Ruth even had a picture of two beavers building a dam. The last was a close-up of a beaver's face.

"Beavers sure are funny-looking," Ava couldn't help saying.

"I agree, but I didn't choose them for their looks," Ruth said, grinning. "I chose them because of how they behave." Ruth's face lit up with excitement. "Beavers are incredible, Ava. They use their body parts like tools to cut down trees and build amazing dams. A beaver dam can change the course of a stream!"

"At least one of us has chosen an animal," Ava thought as she handed the pictures back to Ruth. She was impressed, and even a little jealous. Ruth was so sure about her favorite animal, and beavers were a good choice. Why was Ava having such a tough time choosing one for herself?

"What's your animal?" Ruth asked.

Ava sighed. "I just can't decide," she admitted with a shrug.

Chapter 2: **The Search Begins**

Ruth patted Ava on the shoulder and smiled. "I'm sure you'll find a good one," she said, "because I know how much you love animals." Then she gathered up her pictures and went off to work on her poster.

Ava looked at the clock. She knew she would have only ten minutes to sit at the computer. "Focus," she told herself. But her mind was swirling with ideas. Dolphins might be a good choice. Ava knew they were smart and very playful, like her cat, Minnie. Or what about cats? Ava knew a lot about cats, too.

Ava thought about the big cats at the zoo. The last time she'd been to the zoo, she had taken pictures of them. She'd fed the giraffes, too. Ava loved watching giraffes move their long graceful necks. The pattern on their skin was so pretty. They looked gentle, but strong.

Ava was a bird-watcher, too. She had always wondered what it would be like to fly. She imagined flapping her wings and taking off.

"Is everything okay, Ava?" Mr. Edson asked. Ava was so lost in thought, she hadn't even noticed him standing next to her. Mr. Edson pointed at the clock. "Don't forget you have a time limit."

"I know, Mr. Edson," Ava said. "I won't forget." She thought about asking for his advice, but she knew that she was the only one who could choose her favorite animal.

Mr. Edson nodded and moved on.

Chapter 3: **Diving with Dolphins**

Ava stared at the computer, trying to think. The blank blue screen rippled like water. Which animals liked water? "That's it!" she thought. "Dolphins!" Quickly, she started searching for pictures. She watched a video of dolphins leaping out of the water and imagined swimming with them. "I'd love to swim and play with the dolphins every day," she thought.

"Ava!" Jed's voice interrupted Ava's daydream. "Are you done? It's my turn."

Chapter 4: **Grazing with Giraffes**

"I know," said Ava. "I just need two more minutes, Jed. Please."

"Okay," Jed grumbled.

Ava turned back to the computer. Dolphins were exciting, but maybe giraffes would look more interesting on a poster. Ava found a picture of giraffes stretching their long necks to nibble leaves high in the trees.

Ava drifted into another daydream. She was grazing with a herd of giraffes, swaying her long, graceful neck to reach sweet leaves. "Leaves so sweet are such a treat," she thought. Lost in her fantasy, Ava didn't realize she was actually swaying in her chair with a dreamy smile on her face.

"Ava! Are you all right?" Mr. Edson asked. He sounded concerned.

Ava sat up, startled. "Um, yes," she answered.

"Have you chosen your animal yet? I think your turn is about over," Mr. Edson said.

"I just need a minute," Ava pleaded, turning back to the computer. The giraffe Web site had links to information about other animals, too. Ava clicked on a video about birds.

Chapter 5: **Hunting with Hawks**

Ava watched as a bird of prey with sleek brown feathers circled high above the ground. It was a red-tailed hawk. Ava imagined soaring through the sky, using her keen eyesight to watch the world below. Then the hawk swooped toward the ground and headed straight toward a mouse! Ava's stomach dropped as if she, too, were swooping down.

"AVA!" Mr. Edson's voice shook her out of her daydream. "You can't sit at the computer all day. Other students need to have a turn."

Ava shuddered. "No hawks," she said. "I could never eat a mouse."

"I'm glad to hear it," said Mr. Edson. "Now, you have one more minute. I'm timing you!" He grinned and tapped his watch.

Ava concentrated. Which animal should she choose? "I am being a slowpoke today," she thought. "I'm almost as slow as a turtle." Suddenly, she laughed. "A turtle, of course!" she said. "Turtles are slow but steady, like me." Seconds later, she had a turtle picture printed out. She knew she could find more at home. As Ruth passed by, she gave Ava the thumbs-up sign. "Excellent choice, Ava," Ruth said.

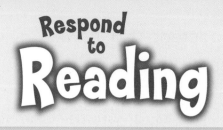

Summarize

Use important details to summarize *Ava's Animals*.

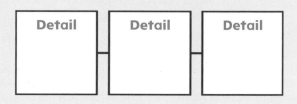

| Detail | Detail | Detail |

Text Evidence

1. How do you know that *Ava's Animals* is fiction?
   GENRE

2. Find a key detail on page 5 that tells why Ruth chose to do her poster on beavers.
   KEY DETAILS

3. What is the meaning of the word *turn* on page 14? Use context clues to help you figure out the meaning. **MULTIPLE-MEANING WORDS**

4. Write about Ava and the kind of person she seems to be. Include a few key details from the story. **WRITE ABOUT READING**

Compare Texts
Read a poem about another animal people love.

Nanook

Nanook the burly polar bear
Loves the Arctic chill.
His playgrounds of white snow and ice
Give him quite a thrill.

Nanook the snowy polar bear
Wears fur to keep him warm.
He doesn't mind the freezing air
And loves a winter storm.

Nanook the big fierce polar bear
Hunts along the shore.
Beluga whales and bearded seals
He truly does adore.

Nanook the giant polar bear
Weighs a ton or more.
When he's angry you can hear him
Grunt and growl and roar.

Nanook the playful polar bear
Splashes in the sea.
He loves to swim in it with friends
Just like you and me.

Make Connections

Why does Ava like turtles? ESSENTIAL QUESTION

How are dolphins like polar bears? TEXT TO TEXT

Focus on
Literary Elements

Rhythm Poems have rhythm, which is a pattern of stressed and unstressed beats. When you read a poem aloud, stressed beats are said with more force. Unstressed beats are said with less force.

What to Look for When you read a poem, listen for stressed and unstressed beats. In the poem below, the stressed beats are in **bold** letters.

Na**nook** the **snow**y **po**lar **bear**
Wears **fur** to **keep** him **warm**.
He **does**n't **mind** the **freez**ing **air**
And **loves** a **win**ter **storm**.

Notice that rhythm is different than rhyme. Some poems, like this one, have both rhythm and rhyme.

Your Turn

Write a short (6-line) rhyming poem. Read your poem a few times to yourself or out loud. Identify the stressed beats. Underline them.